Saltwater Crocodile

The World's Biggest Reptile

by Gabriel Kaufman

Consultant: Meredith Whitney
Herpetology and Conservation Manager
The Maryland Zoo in Baltimore
Baltimore, MD

BEARPORT
PUBLISHING

New York, New York

Credits

Cover, ©Ian D. Walker/Shutterstock; 2–3, ©Daniel Zupanc/Bruce Coleman; 4, Kathrin Ayer; 4–5, ©Ferrero-Labat/ Auscape; 6, ©Mike Parry/Minden Pictures; 7BKG, ©Steven David Miller/Auscape; 8, ©Rainer Drexel/Bilderberg/Peter Arnold; 9, ©James D. Watt/Image Quest Marine; 10 (inset), ©Getty Images; 10–11, ©Jean Paul Ferrero/Auscape; 12, ©Jan Aldenhoven/Auscape; 13, ©Ben & Lynn Cropp/Auscape; 14 (inset), ©Jan Aldenhoven/Auscape; 14–15, ©Frank Woerle/Auscape; 16, ©Breck Kent; 17, ©Jean Paul Ferrero/Auscape; 18, ©Daniel Zupanc/Bruce Coleman; 19, ©Reg Morrison/Auscape; 20–21, ©Mike Parry/Minden Pictures; 22L, ©Jean Michel Labat/Auscape and François Gohier/Auscape; 22C, ©Steven David Miller/Auscape; 22R, ©Kevin Aitken/Peter Arnold; 23TL, ©Rainer Drexel/ Bilderberg/Peter Arnold; 23TR, ©Fritz Poelking/Image Quest Marine; 23BL, ©Juergen Freund/Auscape; 23BR, ©Jean Paul Ferrero/Auscape; 23BKG, ©Jean Michel Labat/Auscape.

Publisher: Kenn Goin
Senior Editor: Lisa Wiseman
Editorial Development: Nancy Hall, Inc.
Creative Director: Spencer Brinker
Photo Researcher: Carousel Research, Inc.: Mary Teresa Giancoli
Design: Otto Carbajal

Library of Congress Cataloging-in-Publication Data

Kaufman, Gabriel.
  Saltwater crocodile : the world's biggest reptile / by Gabriel Kaufman.
      p. cm.—(SuperSized!)
  Includes bibliographical references and index.
  ISBN-13: 978-1-59716-396-5 (library binding)
  ISBN-10: 1-59716-396-1 (library binding)
  1. Crocodylus porosus—Juvenile literature. I. Title.

  QL666.C925K39 2007
  597.98—dc22
                          2006031415

For more information, write to Bearport Publishing Company, Inc., 101 Fifth Avenue, Suite 6R, New York, New York 10003. Printed in the United States of America.

10 9 8 7 6 5 4 3 2 1

Contents

One Big Crocodile. 4

Homes in the Water 6

Hiding and Hunting 8

Lots of Eating 10

Buried in Mud 12

Noisy Babies 14

Big Talkers 16

A Long, Lazy Life. 18

Safety for Crocodiles 20

More Big Reptiles 22
Glossary 23
Index 24
Read More 24
Learn More Online 24

One Big Crocodile

The saltwater crocodile is the biggest reptile in the world.

A male saltwater crocodile is about as long as a great white shark.

Male crocodiles can grow up to 23 feet (7 m) long. Females can grow up to 10 feet (3 m) long.

Homes in the Water

Saltwater crocodiles are found in parts of Australia and Asia.

They live in rivers and swamps.

Sometimes they swim far out to sea to find a place to live.

Some saltwater crocodiles swim more than 600 miles (966 km) in search of a home.

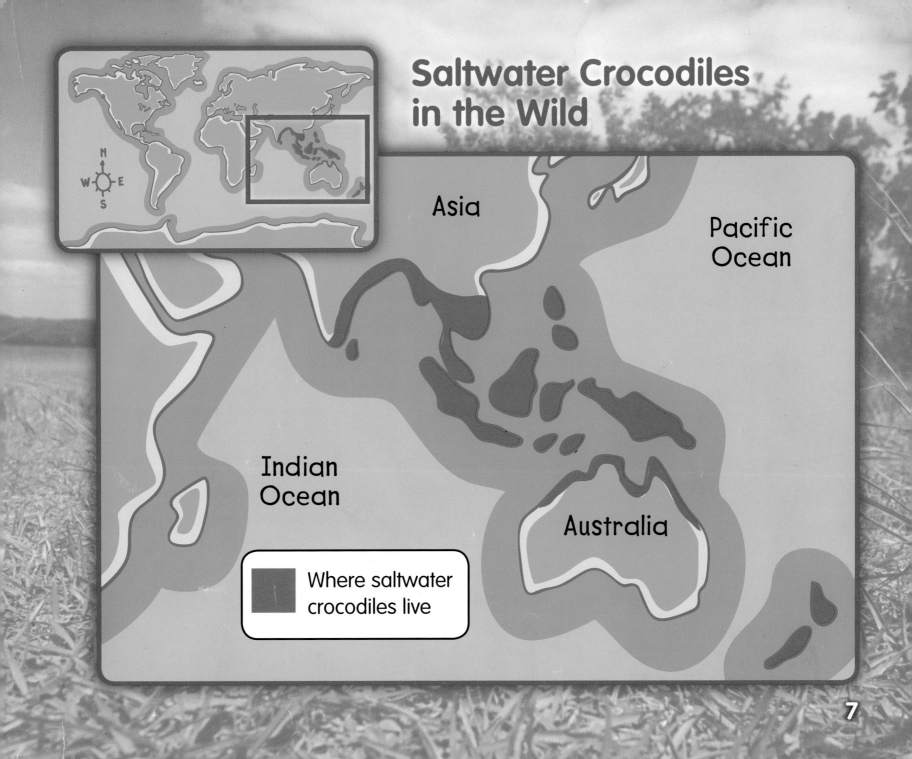

Saltwater Crocodiles in the Wild

Asia

Pacific Ocean

Indian Ocean

Australia

Where saltwater crocodiles live

Hiding and Hunting

A saltwater crocodile hunts for **prey**.

It hides in water.

Only its eyes and **nostrils** show.

When the prey comes close to the water's edge, the crocodile leaps at it.

It grabs the animal with its jaws.

The saltwater crocodile has bigger jaws than any other animal.

Lots of Eating

Saltwater crocodiles hunt many kinds of prey.

Young crocodiles eat insects, fish, and crabs.

Adult crocodiles eat the same animals, too.

crab

Adult crocodiles also catch monkeys, turtles, and wild pigs.

Buried in Mud

Saltwater crocodile mothers lay up to 50 eggs at a time.

They go on shore to bury their eggs in the mud.

The mothers watch over the eggs.

They protect them from other animals.

Saltwater crocodile mothers make good parents. They take care of the babies until they can live on their own.

13

Noisy Babies

Saltwater **crocklets** chirp when they first **hatch**.

The mother crocodile hears her babies' cries.

So she digs them out of the mud.

She carries them in her mouth to the water.

The crocklets are about 1 foot (0.3 m) long when they hatch.

crocklet

Big Talkers

Saltwater crocodiles "talk" to each other by making sounds.

Young crocodiles bark.

Adult crocodiles make deeper barks and growls.

Saltwater crocodiles hiss to warn other animals to stay away.

17

A Long, Lazy Life

Saltwater crocodiles do not move around very much.

Yet when they hunt, they can be very fast.

Saltwater crocodiles live to be about 70 years old.

Safety for Crocodiles

Some people hunt saltwater crocodiles.

They make shoes, wallets, and belts from their skin.

Today, many countries have laws that protect crocodiles.

The laws keep these huge animals safe from hunters.

Crocodiles have lived on Earth for millions of years. They were around even before the dinosaurs.

More Big Reptiles

Saltwater crocodiles belong to a group of animals called reptiles. Most reptiles hatch from eggs. Reptiles are covered with scales. Except for the leatherback turtle, all reptiles are cold-blooded.

Here are three more big reptiles that live in the water.

Nile Crocodile

The Nile crocodile is the biggest crocodile in Africa. It can grow up to 20 feet (6 m) long.

American Alligator

The American alligator can grow up to 14 feet (4.3 m) long.

Leatherback Turtle

The leatherback turtle can grow up to 9 feet (2.7 m) long.

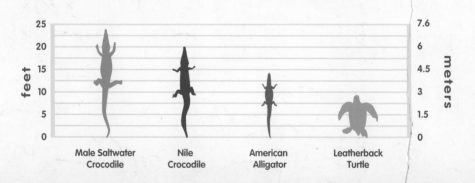

Male Saltwater Crocodile	Nile Crocodile	American Alligator	Leatherback Turtle

Glossary

crocklets
(KROK-lets)
baby crocodiles

nostrils
(NOSS-truhlz)
openings in an
animal's nose
that are used
for smelling and
breathing

hatch
(HACH) to come
out of an egg

prey (PRAY)
an animal that is
hunted by other
animals for food

Index

Africa 22

American alligator 22

Asia 6–7

Australia 6–7

communication 16

crabs 10

crocklets 14

dangers 20

eggs 12, 22

food 8, 10

homes 6–7

hunting 8, 10, 18, 20

jaws 8

leatherback turtle 22

life span 18

mother saltwater crocodiles 12, 14

Nile crocodile 22

prey 8, 10

size 4–5, 14

Read More

Berger, Melvin, and Gilda Berger. *Snap! A Book About Alligators and Crocodiles.* New York: Cartwheel Books (2002).

Fitzgerald, Patrick J. *Croc and Gator Attacks.* New York: Children's Press (2000).

Simon, Seymour. *Crocodiles & Alligators.* New York: HarperTrophy (2001).

Learn More Online

To learn more about saltwater crocodiles, visit **www.bearportpublishing.com/SuperSized**